How to Draw Clifford

Based on the Scholastic book series
"Clifford The Big Red Dog" by
Norman Bridwell

By B.S. Watson

No part of this publication may be reproduced in whole or in part, or stored in a retrieval system, or transmitted in any form or by any means, electronic, mechanical, photocopying, recording, or otherwise, without written permission of the publisher. For information regarding permission, write to
Scholastic Inc., Attention: Permissions Department, 557 Broadway, New York, NY 10012.

ISBN 0-439-54402-5

Designed by Ursula Albano

Copyright © 2003 Scholastic Entertainment Inc. All Rights Reserved. Based on the CLIFFORD THE BIG RED DOG book series published by Scholastic Inc. ™ & © Norman Bridwell. SCHOLASTIC and associated logos are trademarks and/or registered trademarks of Scholastic Inc. CLIFFORD, CLIFFORD THE BIG RED DOG, and associated logos are trademarks and/or registered trademarks of Norman Bridwell.

10 9 8 7 6 5 4 3   04 05 06 07

Printed in the U.S.A.
First printing, December 2003

Somerset County Library
Bridgewater, NJ 08807

SCHOLASTIC INC.

New York Toronto London Auckland Sydney
Mexico City New Delhi Hong Kong Buenos Aires

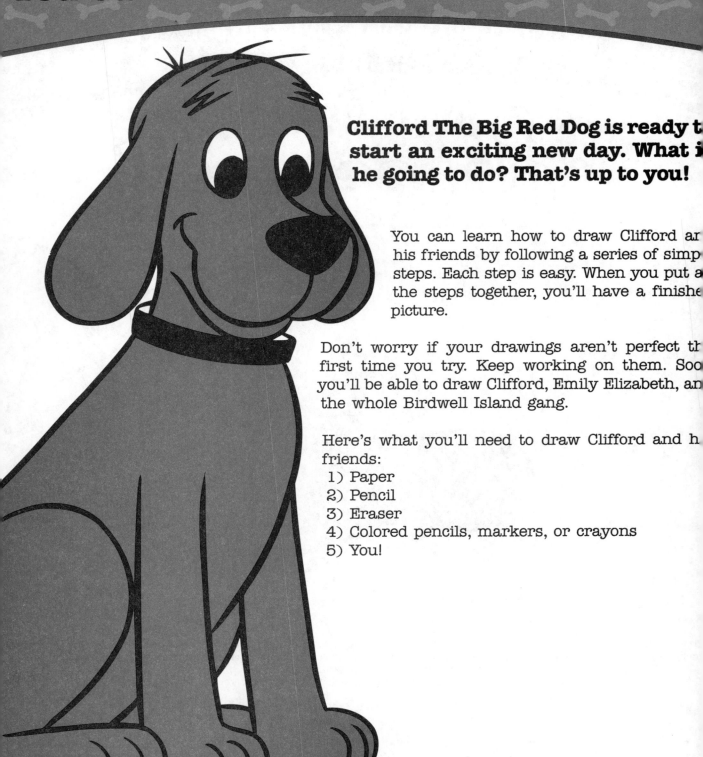

Clifford The Big Red Dog is ready t start an exciting new day. What i he going to do? That's up to you!

You can learn how to draw Clifford ar his friends by following a series of simp steps. Each step is easy. When you put a the steps together, you'll have a finishe picture.

Don't worry if your drawings aren't perfect th first time you try. Keep working on them. Soc you'll be able to draw Clifford, Emily Elizabeth, ar the whole Birdwell Island gang.

Here's what you'll need to draw Clifford and h friends:
1) Paper
2) Pencil
3) Eraser
4) Colored pencils, markers, or crayons
5) You!

Here are a few things you should know before you get started:
1) Draw lightly with your pencil. You can darken your lines later, after you finish your drawing.
2) Stay loose! Don't squeeze your pencil too hard. Let your hand and arm move easily.
3) Follow each step carefully. Take your time and go slowly.
4) Don't worry about mistakes. That's why you have an eraser. Nobody's perfect—not even Clifford!
5) Practice and be patient. Soon you'll be drawing Clifford, Emily Elizabeth, and their friends!

Here are the basic shapes you'll use to draw everything in this book:

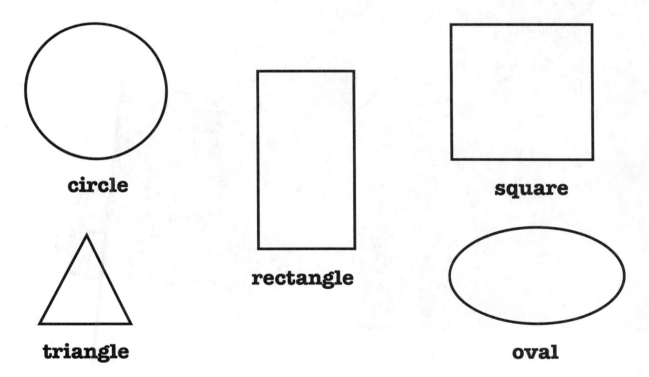

circle

rectangle

square

triangle

oval

Now it's time to start drawing. Ready, set, have fun!

Clifford is the biggest dog around. But his friends are all different sizes, too. When you draw more than one character together, use this guide to see how big each character is compared to the others.

Clifford

Mac   **Cleo**   **T-Bone**   **KC**   **Emily Elizabeth**

Heads up! Everyone loves Clifford The Big Red Dog. And you'll love drawing him, too. Before you learn to draw all of Clifford, start by drawing his head.

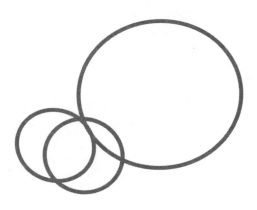

1) Begin by drawing three circles: two small ones and a larger one. The large circle will be Clifford's head. The smaller ones will help form his nose.

2) Add an open-ended oval shape to the side of the large circle. This will be Clifford's ear. Then draw a curvy line from one of the smaller circles. This will help form Clifford's chin.

3) Draw a thin rectangle below the chin. This will be his collar. Now connect the rectangle to the chin and the head with two small lines.

4) Add a triangle for the tip of Clifford's nose and a curved line to form his mouth, as shown.

5) Draw two ovals to form Clifford's eyes. Inside those two ovals, draw two smaller ovals and fill them in. Fill in Clifford's nose, his collar, and his tongue, as shown.

6) Add a few lines of fur to Clifford's head. Then darken your lines. Now erase any extra lines you see on your drawing that are not shown here. Color Clifford red, as shown.

Congratulations! You've drawn Clifford!

Clifford loves to run. Sometimes he even carries his friends on his back as he races along. Here's how to draw Clifford running.

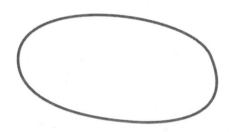

1) Draw an oval.

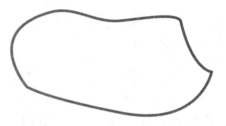

2) Curve the lines of the oval to make the shape you see here. This will be Clifford's body.

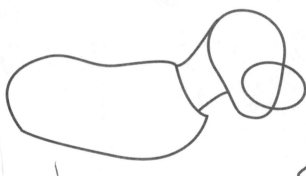

3) Draw two more oval shapes, as shown. These will be Clifford's head and snout. Then connect the head shape to the body shape with two lines.

4) Now it's time to draw Clifford's legs, by adding the lines shown here. Notice how his front legs stretch forward and his back left leg stretches back.

5) In this step, add his tail, add a rectangle for his collar, and add two open-ended ovals for his ears.

6) Draw Clifford's eyes next. Remember that they are made up of two ovals with two smaller ovals inside them. Now draw the triangle for his nose. Fill in the nose, the smaller eye ovals, and the collar. Finish this step by drawing Clifford's mouth.

7) Add a few lines of fur to Clifford's head, then darken all your lines. Erase any extra lines that you don't see here, add color, and you're done!

When Clifford's ready to play, he crouches down and wags his tail happily. Let's draw Clifford in that position.

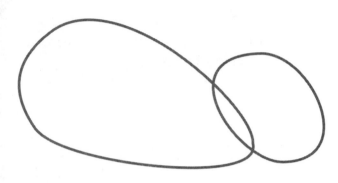

1) Start with two ovals, one for Clifford's body and a smaller one for his head.

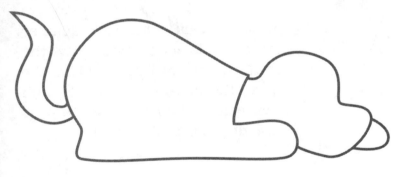

2) Now make the bottom of the body oval flat, and curve the head oval to include Clifford's snout, as shown.

3) In this step, add Clifford's paw just in front of his head. Now draw his tail.

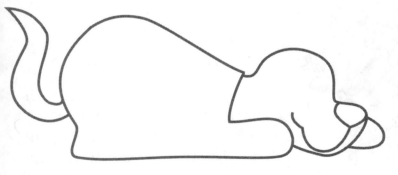

4) Draw a triangle for Clifford's nose. Then draw a curving line from his nose, as shown, to form his mouth. Notice the difference between his mouth in this picture (it's closed) and his mouth in the picture on page 9 (it's open).

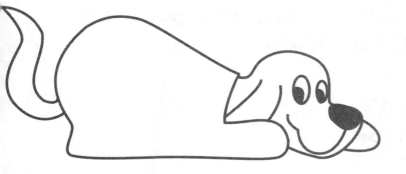

5) Add two sets of ovals for Clifford's eyes and fill in the inner ovals. Then fill in his nose. Now draw two lines toward the back of his head to form his ear.

6) Draw a line for his collar and fill it in. Then draw the curvy lines shown to form his back leg. Draw small lines on Clifford's paws to create his toes.

7) Add a few lines of fur to Clifford's head. To make his tail look like it's wagging, add a couple of small motion lines on either side of his tail. Darken the lines you want to keep, erase the extra lines, and color him in.

Clifford can't wait to see his friends. He's so excited that his tongue sticks out and his floppy ears shake from side to side. You can draw Clifford in this funny pose, too.

1) Begin with a curved oval for Clifford's body, as shown. Then add his head shape. Draw a line to separate the head from the body.

2) Add Clifford's ears and tail.

3) Let's add Clifford's legs. Draw his two front legs using straight lines that round into his paws. Then draw his back leg with a curved line inside the body and a long oval shape below.

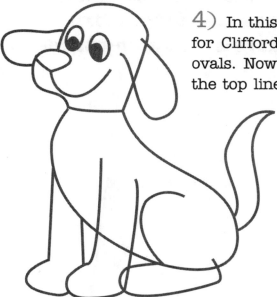

4) In this step, draw two sets of ovals for Clifford's eyes and fill in the inner ovals. Now draw his nose triangle and the top line of his mouth.

5) Fill in Clifford's nose. Add a line for his collar and fill that in, too. Next draw the bottom line of Clifford's open mouth, then draw his tongue. Add his jawline as shown.

6) Add fur lines to Clifford's head. Then add two motion lines next to each of his ears to make it look like he is shaking them. Darken your lines, erase the extra lines, and add color.

Now Clifford is ready to play!

Full of energy and always ready for fun, **T-Bone** is one of Clifford's best friends. Let's learn to draw **T-Bone**, so he can share some adventures with Clifford!

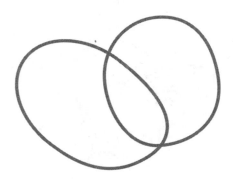

1) Start off by drawing an oval for T-Bone's body and a circle for his head.

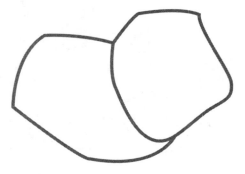

2) Curve the lines so they look like the two shapes shown here.

3) Now add T-Bone's legs. Notice that you can only see a little bit of his back left leg because it's behind his body.

4) In this step, draw T-Bone's tail and ears, as shown.

5) Now add a triangle for his nose, and fill it in. Then draw his mouth shape. Draw two small dots for his eyes. Notice how different T-Bone's eyes are from Clifford's.

6) Fill in part of T-Bone's mouth, as shown. This forms his tongue. Draw two lines above his eyes for his eyebrows. Draw a small circle and a larger half circle on his back for his spots.

7) Add a line around T-Bone's neck for his collar and an oval for his dog tag. Draw small lines on his paws to form his toes (just like you did for Clifford). Darken your lines, erase any extra lines, and color him in, as shown.

Now T-Bone is all set to go find Clifford!

Clifford's friend Cleo may look like a fancy show dog, but she loves to run, jump, and play—just like any other dog! Let's learn to draw her next.

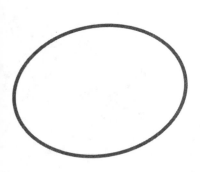

1) Start by drawing a circle for the fur on Cleo's head and a square for the fur around her neck.

2) Change the two shapes so that they look like the shapes shown here.

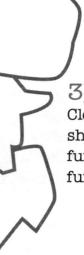

3) Draw the shape for Cleo's face and neck, as shown, connecting the fur on her head to the fur around her neck.

4) In this step, draw Cleo's body and her back right leg. Then draw her remaining three legs.

5) Draw two lines and a roughly shaped oval for Cleo's tail. Draw a small oval for the tip of Cleo's nose, and fill it in. Now draw Cleo's mouth. It's a triangle shape with a curved line at the top. Finally, draw two small dots for her eyes.

6) Here's where Cleo gets fluffy! Draw jagged lines around the fur on her head, chest, and tail. Then draw two small lines across her neck and fill them in to form her collar. Fill in a section of her mouth to form her tongue (just like you did with T-Bone).

7) Draw Cleo's bow using two triangles connected by a rectangle. Add a small line above her eyes (for eyebrows) and lines on her paws for toes. Darken your lines, erase any extra lines, and color her purple, as shown.

Cleo is ready to join Clifford and T-Bone on their next adventure!

KC has only three legs, but that doesn't stop him from playing with the other dogs. Clifford learned from KC that accepting others for who they are leads to great new friends—like KC! Now let's draw him.

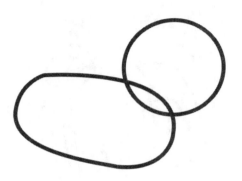

1) Draw an oval for KC's body and a circle for his head.

2) Curve the shapes, as shown here. Don't forget his ear!

3) Now draw KC's three legs. Then add his tail.

4) Now add a triangle for KC's nose and a triangle with a curved line on the top for his mouth.

5) Add two small dots for KC's eyes. Then fill in his nose. Draw his collar using a line around his neck and a small oval shape for the dog tag.

6) Add lines to KC's paws to form toes. Fill in part of his mouth, as you have done with the other characters, to form his tongue. Draw a couple of fur lines on top of his head, plus lines above his eyes for eyebrows.

7) Now draw KC's spots. Start with the shapes you see on KC's back and chest. Then add a small line to his tail. Add the curved line on the left side of KC's face. Darken your lines, erase any extra lines, and add color.

Mac is a bit more serious than most of Clifford's other friends. But he still enjoys playing with Clifford. Let's learn how to draw him.

1) Begin with an oval for Mac's head and a rectangle for his body.

2) Curve the lines and add the back legs, as shown.

3) Add Mac's ears and tail in this step.

4) Draw four straight lines to form Mac's front legs. Add half circles at the bottom for his feet, as shown. Then add his nose triangle and a line for his mouth.

5) Fill in Mac's nose. Add two small dots for his eyes and a small line coming from the bottom of his mouth line to form his chin.

6) Add two lines to form Mac's collar. Darken your lines, erase any extra lines, and color him blue.

Mac is ready to run off and find Clifford!

Emily Elizabeth is Clifford's best friend in the whole wide world. Here's how to draw her.

1) Start by drawing a circle for Emily Elizabeth's head, a rectangle for her body, and long, thin rectangles for her arms and legs. Add ovals for her feet.

2) Change the shapes so that they look like the shapes shown here.

3) In this step, add Emily Elizabeth's hair, as shown. Then draw lines for her shirt collar and a line to separate her shirt from her skirt.

4) Next, draw Emil Elizabeth's hands. Ad a round shape for he ear.

5) Now let's draw her face. Two small dots form her eyes. A curved line forms her nose. Two more lines form her mouth. Add two small lines for her eyebrows.

6) Fill in Emily Elizabeth's shoes next. Draw lines across the center of the top part of her hair. Fill in part of her mouth to form her tongue.

7) Now add two small dots on Emily Elizabeth's shirt to make buttons. Then draw stripes on her socks. Darken your lines, erase any extra lines, and color her in, as shown.

Every dog needs a doghouse, and Clifford is no exception. Let's practice drawing Clifford's doghouse next.

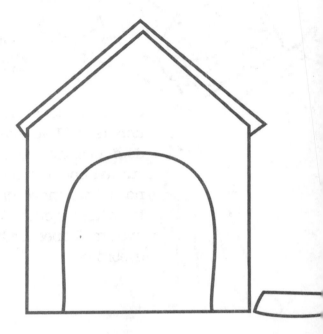

1) Start by drawing a square. Now draw a triangle on top of the square. Add a curved line inside the square, as shown.

2) Add another line just above the top of the triangle to form the roof. Then draw Clifford's dog dish next to the house.

3) Draw a small triangle near the top of the doghouse. Then add the inside lines, as shown.

4) Start to put some of Clifford's stuff inside his doghouse by drawing the shapes you see here.

5) Draw lines on the front of the doghouse to form bricks. Now write Clifford's name on the front of the house. Add details to the items inside the house, as shown.

6) Add a squiggly line along the top of the roof. Then add details to the inside of the doghouse, to the dog dish, and to the triangle vent at the top of the doghouse. Darken your lines, erase any extra lines, and add color, as shown.

Clifford's doghouse is all done!

Cat

1) Draw a circle for the cat's head and an oval for the body, as shown.

2) Now add two triangles for ears. Draw two small shapes for the tail and the paw.

3) Fill in the eyes, nose, and mouth. Add fur, and add lines for the legs and feet, as shown.

4) Finish the cat by adding details to the feet and tail and drawing in some whiskers.

Rabbit

1) Start by drawing an oval for the head and a circle for the body, as shown.

2) Curve the lines, as shown. Add ears, paws, and feet.

3) Add the eyes, nose, and mouth, plus the tail. Then add details to the paws, and draw in eyebrows to complete your drawing.

Seagull

1) Draw an oval and a half circle, as shown.

2) Add the seagull's wings, as shown.

3) Add the eyes, beak, and feet. Complete your drawing by adding details to the wings.

Bone

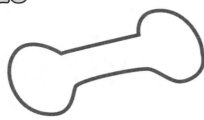

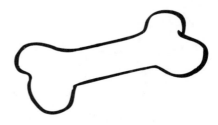

1) Draw the basic bone shape, as shown.

2) Finish up your drawing, as shown here.

Beach Ball

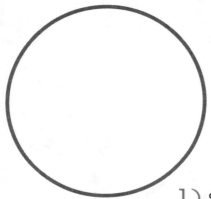

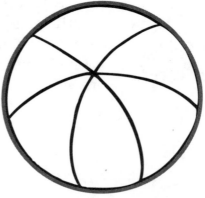

1) Start by drawing a circle.

2) Add curved lines to th circle, as shown.

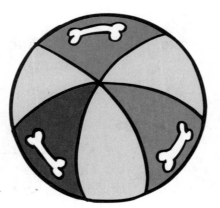

3) Finish your beach ball t drawing three dog bones.

Dog Dish

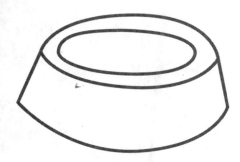

1) Start by drawing two ovals, one inside the other. Then add lines below the oval, as shown.

2) Draw a dog bone on the outside of the bowl. Then add some Tummy Yummies in the bowl.

Ice-Cream Cone

1) Draw a circle resting on top of a triangle, as shown.

2) Draw some squiggly lines to form the ice cream. Then add some crisscrossing lines on the cone.

Go, Clifford, Go!

Clifford and his friends are spending a day in the park. What are they doing there? It's up to you to draw them!

Here's her winning entry in the "What Would You Do With a Big Red Dog?" story and drawing contest!

What Am I Going To Do With a
Big Red Dog
By Jessie Ng

If I have a big red dog I would bring
him to school on a bright sunny day.

I would sit on his back as he walks
along the way.

I might bring him to show and tell if he
doesn't block the doorway.

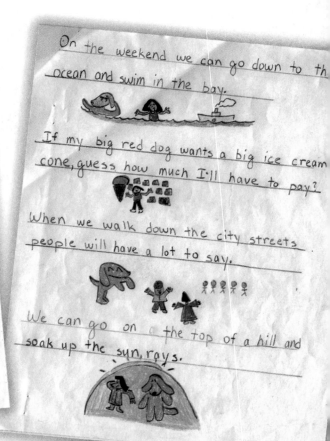

On the weekend we can go down to th
ocean and swim in the bay.

If my big red dog wants a big ice cream
cone, guess how much I'll have to pay?

When we walk down the city streets
people will have a lot to say.

We can go on the top of a hill and
soak up the sun, rays.

And when day turns to night my
big red Dog stopped everyone's
fright.

Because when he scared the robbers
away, everyone shouted "Hurray!!"

J 741.5 WAT   9/20/05
Watson, B. S. (Barry S.)
How to draw Clifford

Watchung Public Library
12 Stirling Road
Watchung, NJ 07069